TO

FROM

DATE

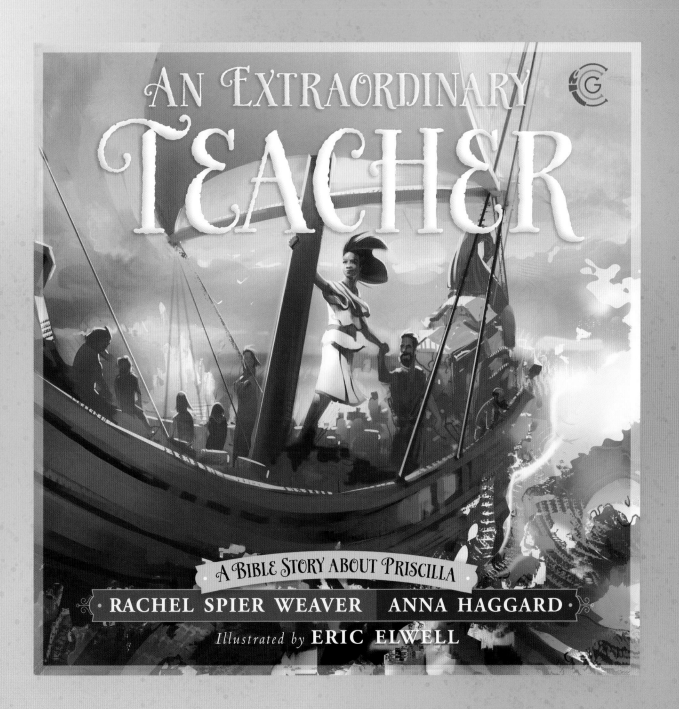

AN EXTRAORDINARY TEACHER

A BIBLE STORY ABOUT PRISCILLA

RACHEL SPIER WEAVER · ANNA HAGGARD ·

Illustrated by ERIC ELWELL

HARVEST HOUSE PUBLISHERS
EUGENE, OREGON 97402
HarvestHousePublishers.com

AN EXTRAORDINARY TEACHER

Text © 2018 by Rachel Spier Weaver and Anna Haggard
Artwork © 2018 by Eric Elwell

Published by Harvest House Publishers
Eugene, Oregon 97408

www.harvesthousepublishers.com

HARVEST KIDS is a registered trademark of The Hawkins Children's LLC. Harvest House Publishers, Inc., is the exclusive licensee of the federally registered trademark HARVEST KIDS.

ISBN 978-0-7369-7081-5 (hardcover)
ISBN 978-0-7369-7082-2 (eBook)

Cover and interior design by Left Coast Design

Published in association with the literary agency of Wolgemuth & Associates, Inc.

Printed in China

17 18 19 20 21 22 23 24 25 26 / LP / 10 9 8 7 6 5 4 3 2 1

Priscilla's Story

Acts 18 • Romans 16:3-5
1 Corinthians 16:9 • 2 Timothy 4:19

Based on the New Testament story, *An Extraordinary Teacher* follows the biblical narrative of the heroine Priscilla, imagining how she responded to the events recorded in Scripture.

Priscilla…PriscillAAAA!"

Priscilla's mother called repeatedly. She couldn't find her daughter, and she was getting worried. The sun was setting, making it difficult to search for Priscilla in the dark.

Then Priscilla appeared, running. Dusty from an afternoon outside, she was carrying a stack of books in her arms, her hair falling from her thick, dark braids.

"Where were you?" Priscilla's mom exclaimed as she her pulled her close.

"I was reading by the gardens!" Priscilla said, breathless. "I'm sorry I lost track of time again—I get lost in the stories!

Priscilla's mom chuckled. Reading was what Priscilla loved most.

Priscilla was one of the lucky girls in Rome who went to school, and she spent many afternoons studying the Torah, the story of God's love for the Jewish people, Priscilla's people.

But Priscilla knew that God had sent his Son Jesus to Earth so that *everyone*—not just the Jewish people—could know God's love! She couldn't keep such good news to herself.

"Priscilla," her mom said as she was tucking Priscilla into bed that night, "Do you know how proud of you I am?"

Priscilla smiled with her nose tucked under the covers. "Why?" she asked

"I hear you teaching your friends about God. You have a gift."

"What do you mean?" Priscilla sat up, leaning on her elbow.

Her mom paused. "God has given you the gift of teaching and has big dreams for you to use your gifts."

Priscilla's heart swelled. As she fell asleep, she wondered how God would call her to teach someday.

As Priscilla grew, she remembered her mother's words; she wanted to be ready when God invited her to use her gifts.

So she studied hard.

No one could equal Priscilla as a scholar—except one boy named Aquila.

"Priscilla, do you want to study with me today?" asked Aquila as they began walking home from school.

"Yes," said Priscilla, "but I'll race you first," she shouted, dashing past him.

Surprised, Aquila took off, closing in just as Priscilla's house came into view.

After that, Aquila and Priscilla studied together
each day. They loved God's Word.

More than anything, they shared a dream to help people know God. When they grew up, they decided to pursue that dream together and got married.

Priscilla and Aquila worked together making roofs for houses and tents for market booths.

"Aquila," Priscilla said with a twinkle in her eye, "let's race!" Aquila grabbed his needles and thread and got to work.

When Aquila had sewn his last stitch, he looked up and saw Priscilla beaming, hands in her lap.

They spent their days racing to see who would be the victor. Sometimes Aquila would win, sometimes Priscilla, but they always had fun together.

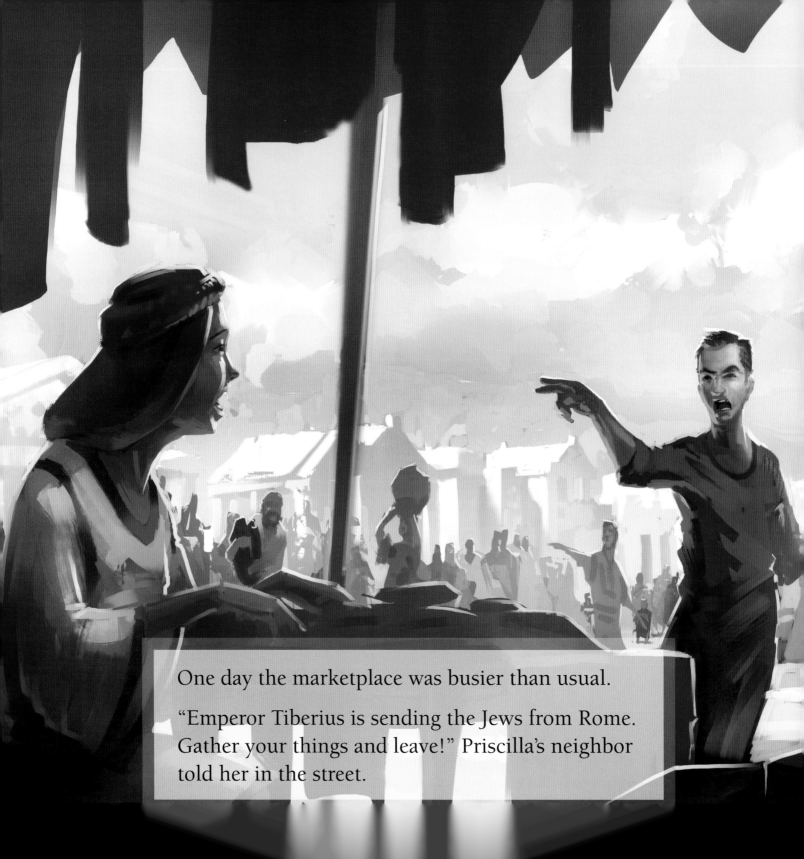

One day the marketplace was busier than usual.

"Emperor Tiberius is sending the Jews from Rome. Gather your things and leave!" Priscilla's neighbor told her in the street.

Priscilla rushed home to tell Aquila, and quickly, they collected everything they owned and headed to the Greek city of Corinth.

Safely away from the emperor, they set up their shop and began to sell tents in the new city.

As they were cleaning up one day, they had a visitor.

"I'm Paul," said a man with a kind face. Before Priscilla could reply, Paul shook her hand. "I hear you make tents," he said with a bright smile. "So do I!"

"Is that right? Sit down and tell us about yourself," said Aquila. That night, Paul shared how he had met Jesus and had been traveling around the world teaching God's love.

"I want the people of Corinth to know that God loves them. Will you join me in telling the good news?" Paul said.

Priscilla and Aquila's hearts stirred. God was calling them to use their gifts!

"We'd love to teach with you," said Priscilla. "Why don't you stay and make tents with us?" Paul accepted.

During long afternoons stitching leather tents together, Paul, Priscilla, and Aquila had exciting discussions about Jesus and Scripture. Just like in school, Priscilla wanted to learn. God had given her a gift, and she passionately prepared herself to teach.

At home in the evenings, the three friends began teaching people about the love of Jesus. Soon their home church was becoming so large they were outgrowing their space.

One evening Paul shared with his friends, "I'm thinking of moving to a new city."

Priscilla's heart fell. She and Aquila would miss Paul dearly.

"But I want to take you and Aquila with me. Would you sail with me to plant a church in Ephesus?"

"*Yes!*" said Aquila and Priscilla together.

Soon the three friends were sailing far away from Corinth, surrounded by nothing but the deep blue sea. During the voyage, the waves crashed fiercely around them.

They fled under the deck to avoid being tossed from the rocking ship.

Praying together, Priscilla, Aquila, and Paul pleaded with God, "Help us reach Ephesus safely!"

The next day, they saw land—Ephesus!

After landing in Ephesus, Paul continued to travel.
Priscilla and Aquila set up a church in their home,
just as they did in Corinth.

Often Priscilla and Aquila preached about Jesus at
the synagogue, where Jews met to worship God.

One day, as they entered synagogue, they heard a deep, booming voice. "My name is Apollos; I studied the Bible for many years in Egypt." Priscilla and Aquila sat down to listen to a towering man whose eyes were alight with passion.

Apollos knew the Scriptures *and* Jesus, just as they did! But Priscilla noticed Apollos was missing a big part of Jesus' story.

"Aquila, Apollos doesn't know that after returning to heaven, Jesus sent the Holy Spirit to be with us all the time! We need to tell him!"

So they invited Apollos for dinner and shared how
the Holy Spirit is like a best friend who always
helps us.

"What amazing news!" Apollos couldn't believe what he was hearing. He stood and wrapped his arms around Priscilla and Aquila. "I can't wait to share how the Holy Spirit is always with us!"

At that moment, Priscilla remembered what her mother had said. "God has given you the gift of teaching and has big dreams for you to use your gifts."

Each stage of her life had prepared her to teach Apollos: working hard in school, studying Scripture with Paul, and teaching and leading in their home churches. God had equipped Priscilla to teach one of the greatest scholars of the early church.

Many came to know Jesus through Priscilla and Aquila. Like Apollos, countless others traveled around the world, sharing what they first learned in Priscilla and Aquila's home church.

Priscilla praised God that God had bigger dreams for her than she could have ever imagined.

· REFLECTION QUESTIONS ·

- What might it have been like for Priscilla and Aquila to leave their home and go to another place?

- Why do you think Paul asked Priscilla and Aquila to go on a missionary journey with him?

- Priscilla had a gift of teaching others about God. What gifts have you been given that you can use to show the love of God?

- Priscilla studied hard so she could be prepared to share God's love with others. What can you do to make sure you're ready to use your gifts for God?

Dear reader,

What Bible stories captured your attention as a child? The stories dramatized on Sunday school felt boards often featured Noah and his ark, David and Goliath, and Paul traveling on his missionary journeys. And rightly so! These stories depict giants of our faith. But the Bible also elevates women—faith-filled adventurers who lead, make brave decisions, and risk everything to follow God. Called and Courageous Girls is a series of children's books that star gutsy biblical women who unleash the kingdom of God.

We are thrilled that you have chosen to read this book in the Called and Courageous Girls series. Our prayer is that these books will provide hours of enjoyable reading, prompt engaging and challenging conversations, and inspire your children to use their talents, passions, and gifts for the kingdom.

Blessings,

Rachel and Anna